TARGET SSB

OIR&PHYCHOLOGY

DIPIKA TIWARI & KULDIP TIWARI

Copyright © Dipika Tiwari & Kuldip Tiwari
All Rights Reserved.

ISBN 979-888606034-8

This book has been published with all efforts taken to make the material error-free after the consent of the author. However, the author and the publisher do not assume and hereby disclaim any liability to any party for any loss, damage, or disruption caused by errors or omissions, whether such errors or omissions result from negligence, accident, or any other cause.

While every effort has been made to avoid any mistake or omission, this publication is being sold on the condition and understanding that neither the author nor the publishers or printers would be liable in any manner to any person by reason of any mistake or omission in this publication or for any action taken or omitted to be taken or advice rendered or accepted on the basis of this work. For any defect in printing or binding the publishers will be liable only to replace the defective copy by another copy of this work then available.

We would like to dedicate this book to all the martyrs of the indian armed forces and especially For our brave soldiers who were martyred on 14 February 2019For our brave soldiers who were martyred on 14 February 2019 pulwama attack.

Contents

Preface

The defence servises offer one of the most challenging and wet meaningfull careers. A soldier is a respected citizen of any country because he/she lives for the vetrues of sacrifiecs commitment selfless devotion ironically though it is such a coveted professior there have been severe shortages in the officer' cadre of the armed forces. while most believe that talented youth do not want to join the armed forces for lack of patriotic favour. It is the dream every armed force's aspirant, to hear their name in the"recommended" list in SSB. Every time a candidate receives call up latter for the ssb, he/she rushes to get the best material to prepare them, to realize there dream. some run on various coaching insititutes, other look up for the books available, while some dig up the internet to get information. Almost all internet sites are modrated by candidates who ones appeared ni the SSBb and do not know the science behind the selection process.With this book we aim to provide the best possible assitance any candidate can expect of. this promoted me to write a book and shere my insight with all the defence aspirants. I have not provide any tips to fool the system. the book divided into four parts. the first part deals with explaining the candidates what SSB is, what are the tasks involved and various other things, which are the unique the books. The second part also contains experieince and interview of the successful candidates the purpose of which is to motivate the candidate and see the SSB from a recommended candidate's perspective. the third part is on of its kind, having exclusive content for the repeaters. this, probably is;the fist book to cover anything of that sort. the fouth part also is rare in a way, as it has the basis level knowledge which a candidate should possess the armed force. it'll be a delight for the readers to find all the content summed up at on place saving them both the time and effort of digging up the innumerable websites on the inernet to collect the information. fourth part also has the sample papers, GK topics,ionformation regarding the coast guard interview process and details of PABT/CPSS test. Ihope that this book will be a fitting help for the candidates preparing for the SSB. this, as of now is the only book which covers all the above mentioned topics the sole purpose behind writing this book is to make the understanding of SSB as well as the preparation of SSB easy for the aspirants. we are thankful to all our followers who have appreciated our work whith this book, we hope to extend our reach to numerous others, and look forward to make SSB a simplified interview.

we extend our warm wishes and all the best to all the aspirants for all their upcoming endeavors. so, what are you waiting for time is limited start now and let's crack SSB together!

CONTENTS

INTRODUCTION

There is a dream which millions see, the dream to work for their motherland. The dream to work amongest the sprawling jets, the thundering guns and the mighty ships. The dream to live and die for their country, the dream to work for the defense forces of india. If you want a career full of adventure, challenge and satisfaction,you are made for it. Indian defense has basically four service under it, Indian Army, Indian Air Force, Indian Navy And Indian Coast Gaurd. In order to join these forces as an officers, you have to pass a tes called Service Selection Board or as we'll refer to it, SSB. It is more or less the same procedure for the former three services, while for the latter one, this procedure differs a little. This book is dedicated to cover all that it needs to get through this test called SSB. This book will be a complete guide from top to bottom about SSB. These institutions are looked up to by everyone for several virtues like discipline,dedication, commitment, adeventure, ets.These institutions provide a very clear and healthy environment to work and live in with a sense of pride and honour. If the yester years, only the elite sections of society could join the service as officers and it was a matter of prestinge to be associated with the Armed force. How ever, post the 1990's, the laster of working abroad your working in multinational companies and earning hug sums of money diverted the youth to this last lustrous jobs and fewer numbers aspired to join the defense forces. How ever within a span of to decades, realilty has dawned upon our youth and the latest trend is the engineers working in the best of companies like TCS,WIPRO,ets. As piri fpr defence careers. Thus the armed forces have stood the test of time.

Highlights Of Career As An Officer

* As an officer one enjoys a great sense of purpose of serving the motherland.

* Wearing the uniform gives a sense of pride and honour.

* Opportunity to lead a large team at a very young age.

* Fantstic camaraderie and teamwork.

* Desciplined and orderly life stage.

* Best of traning and education.

* Sport and adventure.

Work- life balance and overall Well-Being.reding up

What we are talking about?

For those of you who have no idea about SSB, and have picked up this book from some recommendation, it is necessary to give a simple and brief introduction. also, if you are a veteran in SSB, there is no harm in reading up a little and clearing up your mind. So, to begin with, as mentoined, to become an officer in the defence forces of india, you need to pass an interview called SSB. No matter which service and which branch you are applying for, SSB is a must, Except for the medical branch in each service.

This book will focus on the procedure of SSB for Army, Navy and Air Forces. procedure for selection in Coast Gaurd differs a little. There are a number of selection boards where the SSB takes place. There might be one or more than one board in one location. If there is more than one board at a single location they are together termed as selection center. There are three selection center, currently existing, which contain a number of boards for Army and Navy, Air Forces has five selection boards. Each board is genrally referred by number

Army - 11SSB, 14 SSB, 18SSB, 19SSB, 34SSB, - Selection center East(SCE) - Allahabaad, UP

Army - 20SSB, 21SSB, 22SSB, - Selection center Central(SCC) - Bhopal, MP

Army - 17SSB, 24SSB, - Selection center South(SCS) - Banglore, Karnataka

Army - 31SSB, 32SSB, - Selection center North(SCN) - Kapurthala, Punjab

Navy - 33SSB - Selection center Central(SCC) - Bhopal, MP

Navy - 12SSB - Selection center South(SCS) - Banglore, Karnataka

Navy - NSB - - - - - - Coimbatore, Tamil Nadu

Navy - NSB - - - - - Navshakti Nagar, Vizag, Andhra Pradesh

Air Force - 1AFSB - - - Dehradun, Uttarakhand

Air Force - 2AFSB - - - Mysore, Karnataka

Air Force - 3AFSB - - - Gandhinagar, Gujarat

Air Force - 4AFSB - - - Varanasi, UP

Air Force - 5AFSB - - - Kanchrapara, West Bengal

so now you are all equipped with the information pon where the SSB takes place. The board consists of different officers, and he headed by one officer, who is fairly senior in rank, know as the president of the board. The people who comprise the board are the commissioned officers, trained for the purpose of selection, with an exception of the psychologist, who may be a civilian.

How to apply for SSB?

SSB is not like a genral test for which you can simply enroll yourself. to reach the stage of SSB, you need to apply first. There are basically two modes of entry through which you can reach the procedure of SSB, Direct and Indirect.

Direct Entry:

In this mode you don't have to give any written tests. All you need to do is simply fill up the form, which is generally online and provide cuttoff percentage decided by the concerned authority and candidate who have higher percentage than the cutoff in their course, based on which they are applying, are called for SSB. Examples for this entry are the entries of Navy, TGC Army, SSC-TechArmy etc.

Indirect Entry:

In the entries of such type, you have to pass a written examination. The cutoff for the score in the examination is decided and the candidates scoring above the cutoff are called for SSB. Examples of such entry include AFCAT, CDSE and NDA.

All these entries have associated eligibilities with them. Genrally, they have a set time of the year for these entries to come. A complete list Regarding all the entries of the forces is given on our book. You may look at them and keep a check in order to apply on time.

What is SSB?

SSb is a six day interview, conducted to find out the suitability of a candidate for the Armed Forces of India. This interview comprises of a number of tests, which are designed such that they check the "Officer Like Qualities (OLQ)" of a candidate. In order to be inducted as an officer, a candidate must prossess certain OLQ's. We'll be taking about OLQ's in drtail in the next section. SSB interview is spread over a period of six days. Here are the features of SSB interview, which make it aunpque interview:

* It is process of six days, in a stretch, without break.

* Boarding and loading facility is provided by the board itself.

* once the candidate is selected, he/she is said to be arecommended by the board, the final seelection is subject to the medical fitness of the candidate and the merit list

*SSB is about the right fit and not the best fit, so a candidate must prosess certain OLQ;s in order to get selected.

* pickup and drop the railway station, in which board the is located , is also provided by the board to the candidates. Travel fare of three-tier AC is given to candidates going for the first time.

* The testing is done in two phases, the Phase 1 testing conducted on the first/second day, and the candidates who clear it are retained for phase two testing, for the remaining days.

* Phase two consits of three types of testing, about which we'll talk in detail later.

* SSB is about the right fit, and not the best fit, so a candidate must prossess certain OLQ's in order to get selected.

* Once the candidate is selected, he/she is said to be a recommended by the board, the final selection is subject to the medical fitness of the candidate and the merit list.

*Once you report for SSB at the railway station, you are taken to the selection board. once inside the selection board, your mobile phones and any other devices like laptops, plamtops and tablets are submitted to the board, which ypu get only when ypour SSB is over.

Testing Schedule;

Unlike other organisations, the selection process in the armed forces is very elaborate and is done over five days. Three different assessors, namely the Interviewing Officer, Group Testing Officer and the Psychologist, test each candidate from three different perspectives and arrive at their respective decisions. Thereafter, on the last day in the board conference, they all sit together and discuss each case to arrive at the final decision. The schedule of testing is described below.

Reporting Day–

Normally, candidates are made to report in the afternoon and are picked up by a bus from the railway station. On reporting, they are given an opening briefing by the duty GTO covering the testing schedule, dos and don'ts, etc. After that, the candidates are asked to fill up a Personal Information Questionnaire (PIQ) form. The PIQ forms the basis of psychological testing and the interview. The importance of this form and how to go about filling this are covered later.

Day 2–

Candidates are put through a screening test which comprises intelligence tests followed by a picture perception and discussion test. Based on the performance in these tests, some of the candidates are retained for stage 2 testing and others are allowed to return home the same day. Hence, qualifying in this test is most important.

Day 2–

On day 2, candidates screened in on day 1 are put through psychological tests which comprise Word Association Test (WAT), Thematic Apperception Test (TAT) and Situation Reaction Test (SRT). In addition, the candidates are asked to describe themselves (Self-Description). On completion of these tests, the interview will start.

Day 3–

Candidates go through Group Testing on day 3 and 4. They are divided into groups of 6 to 10 each depending upon the total candidates screened in. On day 3, Group Discussion (GD), Group Planning Exercise (GPE), Progressive Group Task (PGT), Group Obstacle Race (GOR), Half Group Task (HGT) and Lecturette are conducted. In some cases, even the Individual Obstacles can be conducted on day 3 itself depending upon the weather and engagements of the assessor. On completion of the GTO testing, the interviews of the remaining candidates are done.

Day 4–

On day 4, the remaining tasks of the Group Testing like Individual Obstacles, Command Task and Final
Group Task are conducted. On completion of group testing, interviews of the remaining candidates are
done.

Day 5–

The last day is the conference day wherein each candidate is called in one by one for a final look and a final decision is arrived at. The results are announced by afternoon and candidates not recommended are allowed to leave.

Day 6 to 10 –

Successful candidates are put through medicals in the nearest military hospital and on an average, it takes five days to complete. Those who fail in the medicals are allowed to appeal to the nearest military hospital within 45 days.

OLQ's Redefined:

Candidates often asked me at the end of all the tests what the assessors look for at the time of selection. It is unfortunate that they do not even know what are they tested for. This chapter will deal with the 15 Officer Like Qualities (OLQs), arranged in four factors, that are assessed in the SSBs. Incidentally, all three assessors measure the same 15 qualities using their respective tools/techniques as described in the later chapters. Hence, it is important for the candidates to know what is seen at the SSB.

Factor I: Planning and Organising

This factor includes four qualities which are associated with the mental aspect of the person.

1. *Effective Intelligence (EI):*

This is the ability of a person to evolve solutions to practical problems. It is different from basic
intelligence which is measured using the intelligence tests (Verbal and Non-Verbal). In EI, the assessor wants to see if you can solve day-to-day problems and cope with the minor difficulties of daily life. 2.

Reasoning Ability (RA):

It is the ability of a person to grasp a given situation and arrive at a conclusion by rational thinking. In RA, the assessors are looking for your receptivity, inquiring attitude, logical reasoning and the ability to see the essentials of a problem.

3. Organising Ability (OA):

It is the ability to use resources systematically to produce effective results. In OA, the assessors are interested in seeing how you use the various resources to produce results.

4. Power of Expression (POE):

It is the ability to put across one's ideas adequately and with ease and clarity.

Factor II: Social Adjustment

This factor includes three qualities which are associated with the heart/conscience of the person.

5. Social Adaptability (SA):

It is the ability of a person to adapt himself/herself to the social environment and adjust well with persons and social groups. The assessor is interested in your abilities to adapt to the members of the group, how you interact with them and with the assessor, are you tactful in your dealings with others, etc.

6. Cooperation (Co):

It is the attitude of an individual to participate willingly and in harmony with others in a group to achieve the group goal. It is important to be a team player and one must not be selfish. The group aim and objectives should be most important as compared to individual aims and objectives. The assessors will be keen on seeing your team attitude.

7. Sense of Responsibility (SOR):

It is the thorough understanding of the values of duty, social standard, and of whatis expected of an individual and then giving it one's energy and attention on one's own accord. The assessor is keen on knowing if you understand your duty as a child/student/citizen of a country and whether you have a right sense of what is the social standard and know what is expected of you as an individual, and then whether you give your best energy and attention towards it without anybody having to remind you or tell you. For example, if as a student you have not done well in school/college and do not have a valid reason for poor performance, it will be interpreted as a low sense of responsibility. Because, as a student, your duty is to study hard, and if you have failed to do that, it will obviously mean that your sense of responsibility is low.

Factor III: Social Effectiveness

This factor includes five qualities which are an outcome of the dynamic interaction of the above two factors, i.e. the head and the heart.

8. Initiative (Inv):

It is the ability to originate an action. The assessors see if you take the lead in the right direction and
sustain it till the result is achieved.

9. Self-confidence (SC):

It is the faith in your own abilities to meet stressful and unfamiliar situations.

10. Speed of Decision (SOD):

It is the ability to arrive at a workable decision quickly. There are two components of this, namely, appropriateness of the decision and quickness in arriving at a decision.

11. Ability to Influence the Group (AIG):

It is the ability of aperson to influence others in the group to achieve the objectives set by him/her. What is seen is, whether you can convince others to do things that you want them to do willingly, without the use of any force.

12. Liveliness (Liv):

It is the capacity of a person to remain calm and cheerful when faced with difficulties, and bring about a cheerful atmosphere in the group. What is seen is, whether you get unduly worried or disturbed when faced with difficult situations.

Factor IV: Dynamism

This factor includes three qualities which are associated with thelimbs or the coordination between the mind and the body.

13. Determination (Det):

It is the ability to put in sustained efforts to achieve objectives in spite of obstacles and setbacks. The assessors see whether you are focused, able to concentrate on the task and continuously work towards achieving the objectives.

14. Courage (Cou):

It is the ability to appreciate and take purposive risks. What is important is to take risks only where required and that too after careful thought. Some candidates tend to make rash decisions which may endanger the life of subordinates and that is undesirable. Hence, what is important is 'calculated risks
when required'.

15. Stamina (Sta):

It is the capacity to withstand protracted physicaland mental strain. It includes both physical and mental
endurance.In the subsequent chapters, a brief description of how assessment of these qualities is done will be discussed.

Even though officially, only 15 OLQs are tested, there is an unstated quality which is of great interest to the assessors, namely the "Urge and

Motivation" of the candidate. Hence, your zeal in pursuing a military career is extremely important.

Personal Information Questionnaire (PIQ)

PIQ is a very important document to be filled up on your arrival. The information that you furnish becomes the basis for the Interview. Any mismatch between the information written in the PIQ and what you say during the interview can be viewed very critically. For example, if you write in the PIQ that your favourite sport is basketball and it is found later during the interview that you play some other game and do not know much about basketball, then it is not a very good situation. Hence, what you write in the PIQ is very important and requires a lot of deliberation. The PIQ format is given below for guidance. Carefully read the same and fill it in such a way that whatever you write in this is maintained during the interview and you are prepared to answer questions about some of the information in the PIQ. For example, if you write your hobby as 'reading', then you must know the author and publisher of some of the books that youhave read recently.

Personal Information Questionnaire

1. Name (in capital letters):
....(as in the
Application Form)
2. Father's Name:

....

3. Place of maximum residence:

....

4. Present Address (with approximate population of the city/town/village):

....

....

....

....

5. Permanent Address (with approximate population of the
city/town/village):

....

....

....

....

6. Fill in the details below:
a. State & District :

....

b. Religion :

....

c. Whether SC/ST/OBC :

....

d. Mother Tongue :

....

e. Date of Birth :

....

f. Parents alive :

....

g. If not, your age at the time of father's/mother's death :

....

7. Parents'/Guardians' Occupation/Income (as applicable):
Particulars Education Occupation Income per month
(i) Father ....
(ii) Mother ....
(iii) Guardian ....
8. Educational Record (Commencing from Matriculation)
Exam Year
Div &
Marks

Medium of
Instruction

Boarder/Day
Scholar

(i) Matric/Hr Sec
(ii) 10+2 Equivalent
(iii)
BA/B.Sc./B.Com./BE
(iv) Professional
9. (a) No. of Brothers

....

(b) No. of Sisters

....

(c) Your No. in Siblings

....

10. Age (Years+Months) .... Height (in
metres)................................ Weight (in kg)
....
11. Present Occupation and personal monthly income, if any

....

12.
(a) NCC Training : Yes/No

(b) Total Trg (if any, give
details) :

Total Training –

....

Wing – ....
Division – ....
Certificate Obtained –

....

13. (a) Participation in games & sports:

....

....

....

....
....
....
....

(b)
Hobbies/Interests:...
....
....
....
....
....
....
....

(c) Participation in **extra-curricular activities:**

....
....
....
....
....
....
....

(d) Position of responsibility/Offices held in NCC/Sports/ Extra-
curricular Group and other fields:

....
....
....
....
....
....

Pilot Aptitude Battery Test (PABT)

All candidates aspiring to become pilots are put through a battery of tests to check if they have the aptitude to be a pilot. This is a mandatory test for all candidates wanting to be a pilot irrespective of their choice of service. PABT is conducted only at Air Force Selection Boards (AFSB), and even if the candidate wants to join the Army/Navy, he will be sent to one of the AFSBs for PABT as only the Air Force has this facility. Earlier, candidates were not put through any such tests. However, during World War II, the NATO forces realised that not all pilots were successful on the job and that there were many accidents and crashes. Resultant research suggested that to be a successfulmilitary pilot the person should have certain innate attributes like agility, good reflexes, judgement, presence of mind and nerve to withstand severe mental and physical strains. This resulted in the development of PABT. It is believed that if a candidate does not have the aptitude naturally, he cannot be trained on these and hence, a candidate who fails in these tests once is permanently rejected to be a pilot and no second chance is given to him/her. It is in the interest of both the candidate and the service not to take chances with such a high-risk profession. Hence, across the country, no coaching is available for this test.

Even though one cannot be trained for PABT, it could be of some use to know the procedure and the various tests that are done so that the candidate is prepared mentally to approach the test. PABT includes the following:

*Written test based on instrument reading

*Light control test based on sensory-motor apparatus

*Drum test to check control of velocity

Instrument Reading Test

Aircraft have several instruments that indicate various para meter which the pilot is required to monitor. This test is to see if thecandidate can read the instruments and make mental calculations.Each instrument used in the test is described briefly in the subsequent paragraphs.

Magnetic Compass (Gyroscope):

This gauge indicates the direction of the flight. It has a suspended needle that always points towards true North and with respect to the true North, one can read the direction in which the aircraft is flying.

Air Speed Indicator:

This instrument provides the speed of the air, which is a vital parameter for flying operations. This instrument will provide the indicated Air Speed that is required to be corrected for certain instruments and positional errors to arrive at True Air Speed in kilometres or miles.

Altimeter:

This instrument provides the height at which the aircraft is flying. It is measured in feet or yards. This instrument has three needles like a wristwatch. Of this, the smallest needle indicates height in multiples of 10,000 feet, the middle needle indicates height in multiples of 1,000 feet and the larger needle indicates height in multiples of 100 feet.

Artificial Horizon:

This instrument provides a reference in terms of the horizon for indicating climb, descent, right turn and
left turn of the aircraft.

Turn Indicator:

This instrument indicates the turn on either side of the aircraft. In turning left, the black ball remains in the middle and the white needle moves right, and when turning right, the needle shifts to the left.

Climb and Descent Indicator:

This instrument indicates the position of the aircraft in terms of climb or descent. When the aircraft is climbing, the needle moves upwards and when the aircraft is descending, the needle moves down.

Light Control Test

In this test, the candidate is made to sit in front of a CRT monitor. The chartered path of the flight is defined in that and the candidate is asked to fly along the chartered path by keeping the light which represents the aircraft on the monitor, on the chartered path. The instrument will simulate real-time situations of losing height, tilting, etc., and the candidate is expected to control the aircraft using the joystick, foot pedals and lift lever, which are similar to actual controls available on-board an aircraft.

Drum Test

This is another test to check the control/motor skills of the candidate. In this, there is a drum of about eight feet length and one foot diameter. There are lines marked on the surface of the drum with some holes on each line. The candidate is given a knob to control, which is very sensitive. The drum is rotated and the candidate is expected to align the knob with the lines on the drum as it rotates. Since the knob is very sensitive, it is not so easy to do this. Only candidates who have very good reflexes will be able to do it. This aptitude is required to maintain the flight under normal and turbulent weather conditions when the wind velocity disturbs the flight trajectory and even causes the flight to lose height suddenly.

While the above tests have been described to some extent, it is not possible to explain the entire process as it is very unconventional and unfamiliar. Further, there is no way that a candidate can practise and improve his performance and hence, it suffices to know the broad details of this test.

More recently, the conventional PABT has been replaced by a computer-based system called the CPSS. However, the tests remain the same, except that they are computerised and are no longer conducted using a pencil-paper format.

Section 1 – OIR

Intelligence Tests (Verbal)

Introduction

Normally, SSBs call around 300 candidates per batch, of which around one-third report for testing. The entire lot is put through Stage 1 testing, which comprises Intelligence Tests (Verbal and Non-Verbal) followed by a Picture Perception and Discussion Test (PP&DT). The intelligence tests are similar to IQ tests conducted in any admission/entrance exam and many of them are available on the internet and in other IQ test books. Based on your performance in these two tests, your Intelligence Rating is derived and this, put together with your performance in the PP&DT, will decide your selection for the second stage testing. To give you an idea of the same, a few sample tests are given below with their solutions.

These tests usually involve grammar, verbal analogies, synonyms, antonyms, etc. Because they depend on understanding the precise meaning of words, idioms and the structure of the language, they requiren practice and regular reading of newspapers and books. This test may contain anywhere between 30 to 60 questions and, depending upon the number of questions and their difficulty level, the time allowed to attempt it will vary. You will usually find questions on all of the following:

** Spelling*
** Grammar*
** Sentence Completion*
** Analogies*
** Word Groups*
** Instructions*
** Critical Reasoning*
** Verbal Deductions*

Examples of each of the above categories are provided as illustrations and thereafter, some sample tests are provided with answers for practice.

Spelling Questions

1. Which of the following words are incorrectly spelt?
A. Separate
B. Ordnance
C. Success
D. None of these
2. Choose the pair of words that best completes the sentence:
The ___________ of the timetable caused some ___________
(A) rivision (A) inconvenince
(B) revision (B) inconvenience
(C) revission (C) inconvenence
(D) revition (D) inconveneince

Spelling Questions
1. Which of the following words are incorrectly spelt?
A. Separate
B. Ordnance
C. Success
D. None of these
2. Choose the pair of words that best completes the sentence:
The ___________ of the timetable caused some ___________
(A) rivision (A) inconvenince
(B) revision (B) inconvenience
(C) revission (C) inconvenence
(D) revition (D) inconveneince

Spelling Questions
1. Which of the following words are incorrectly spelt?
A. Separate
B. Ordnance
C. Success

D. None of these

2. Choose the pair of words that best completes the sentence:

The ___________ of the timetable caused some ___________

(A) rivision (A) inconvenince

(B) revision (B) inconvenience

(C) revission (C) inconvenence

(D) revition (D) inconveneince

Answers

1. B 2. B

Missing Word Questions

These questions are designed to measure your vocabulary, specifically your understanding of precise word meanings. You will usually be offered a choice of four or five words, any of which could complete the sentence. These questions are relatively straightforward but because more than one of the words will
complete the sentence satisfactorily, you must read it carefully and choose the best word.

Example Questions

Which of these words completes the sentence in a way that makes most sense?

3. A spirit-level should be used to ensure that the surface is
____

A. Straight

B. Flat

C. Horizontal

D. Parallel
E. Aligned
4. He avoided ___________ because he was ___________
A. Redundant
B. Indispensable
C. Redundancy
D. Indispensible

3. C 4. CB 5. CD

Related Word Questions

To answer this, you need to understand word relationship or a precise meaning of the words in the question and establish what exactly the relationship is between them. You should then look at the answer options and decide which one is the most appropriate. These questions test your reasoning ability as well as your vocabulary.

Example Questions

Which of these is the missing word?
6. Kick, ___________, walk
A. Throw
B. Toes
C. Shin
D. Feet
E. Hand
7. Key, ___________, walk

A. Lock
B. Stand
C. Board

D. Fob

E. Stone

8. Water, _______________, over

A. Ice

B. Derive

C. Wet

D. Flow

E. Fall

Answers

6. D - Feet are used for both kicking and walking
7. C - Board forms the words 'keyboard' and 'boardwalk'
8. E - Fall forms 'waterfall' and 'fall over'.

Synonym and Antonym Questions

These are words which have either the same or opposite meanings. Once again, these word meaning questions test your vocabulary— you need to know the precise meaning of the words given in order to select the appropriate synonym (same meaning).

Example Questions

9. Which two of these words are opposite in meaning?

A. Lose

B. Winner

C. Victor

D. Loser

E. Vanquish

10. Which of these words is the odd one out?
A. Swindle
B. Harass
C. Provoke
D. Annoy
E. Pester

11. Which of these words is the odd one out?
A. Verify
B. Authenticate
C. Confirm
D. Ask
E. Substantiate

Answers

9. BD - Are exact opposites
10. A - The others are synonyms
11. D - The others are synonyms

Word Pair Questions

Firstly, you need to establish the relationship between 'X is to Y' words before you can arrive at the answer. Some people find it helpful to mentally express the relationship before they look at the answer option. This can short-circuit the process of considering and rejecting each option because you know in advance exactly what you are looking for.

Example Questions

12. Dog is to canine as wolf is to ___________
A. Vulpine

B. Ursine
C. Piscine
D. Bovine
E. Lupine

13. Sadness is to happiness as defeat is to ___________
A. Joy
B. Victory
C. Tears
D. Victor
E. None of these

14. Paper is made from timber, as ___________ is made from hide
A. Tree
B. Seek
C. Ox
D. Animal
E. Leather

Answers

12. E 13. B 14.E

Comprehension Questions

These questions consist of a short passage and some related questions. They will often be about a topic which is unfamiliar to you, but this is an advantage rather than a disadvantage because you need to answer the questions based only on the information that you are given—not using any knowledge that you already have. Most people find the best way to tackle these verbal comprehension questions is to scan the text fairly quickly to get a general idea and then attempt each question in turn, referring back to the appropriate part of the text.

Example Question

15. Read the following short passage and say whether or not the statements are true.

There are seven species of deer living wild in Britain. The Red Deer and the Roe Deer are native species. Fallow Deer were introduced by the Romans and, since the seventeenth century, have been joined by three other non-native species: Sika, Muntjac and Chinese Water Deer, which have escaped from parks. In addition, a herd of Reindeer was established in Scotland in 1952. Most of the Red Deer in Britain are found in Scotland, but there are significant wild populations in southwest and northwest England, East Anglia and the north Midlands. Red Deer can interbreed with the introduced Japanese Sika deer and in some areas, hybrids are common.

i. All of the Red Deer in Britain are found in Scotland.
(A) True (B) False (C) Can't say

ii. Red Deer can interbreed with Fallow Deer.
(A) True (B) False (C) Can't say
iii. The Fallow Deer is not native to Britain.
(A) True (B) False (C) Can't say
iv. There are no Reindeer in England.
(A) True (B) False (C) Can't say

Answers

i. B ii. C iii. A iv. C*

*Note that you must answer these verbal comprehension questions using only the information supplied. Red Deer cannot interbreed with Fallow Deer but, because this is not stated in the text, you must answer 'can't say' even if you know that the statement is technically false.

Reasoning Questions

These questions are not concerned with measuring your fluency in English. They are designed to test your ability to take a series of facts expressed in words and to understand and manipulate the information to solve a specific problem.

Example Question

16. Working together, Tom, Dick and Harry need 9 hours to paint a 400-metre-long fence. Working alone, Tom could complete the task in 18 hours. Dick cannot work as fast and needs 36 hours a paint the fence by himself. If Tom and Dick take the day off, how many hours will it take Harry to paint the fence by himself?

(A) 9 (B) 12 (C) 18 (D) 36

Answers

D – In 9 hours, Tom would have painted half of the fence and Dick would have painted one quarter of it. This leaves one quarter to be painted by Harry who must work at the same speed as Dick.

Coding-Decoding

Coding is a method of transmitting a message between the sender and the receiver that no third person can understand. These questions are designed to test your mental ability to grasp the logic and decode the coded Wordes.

Examples

17. If 'ZYXW' is coded as 'ABCD', then 'STUV' will be coded as

Answer

Z – A, Y – B, X – C, W – D
V – E, U – F, T – G, S – H
STUV = HGFE

18. If 'bcd' is coded as 'def', then 'True' is coded as

Answer

b – d (+2) c – e (+2) d – f (+2)

+2 letters are considered in this code.
True – Vtwg

19. If 'Hyderabad' is coded as 'Ixedszcze', then 'Chennai' is coded as.

Answer

H – I (1+), Y – X (1–), D – E (1+), E – D (1–) R – S (1+),
A – Z (1–), B – C (1+), A – Z (1–), D – E (1+)
∴ Chennai → dgfmozj

Section 2 – Psychological Tests

Thematic Apperception Test (TAT)

How the test is conducted

In this test, 12 pictures are shown one by one and candidates are asked to write a short story based on these pictures. The first picture will appear for 30 seconds and thereafter 4 minutes are allowed to write the story in about 100 words, after which the second picture will appear on the screen. The last picture is always a blank slide. Hence, the candidate can write any story and therefore should prepare a nice story for the last picture. The rest of the stories must be purely based on the pictures shown.

Points to Remember

The pictures can be perceived in a hundred different ways. But remember that the main character in the story is actually 'you'. Whatever you write about the main character is actually how you will behave in life. A series of pictures and sample stories are given below as illustration. After each story, a note has been provided to highlight how the desired traits have been projected through then stories.

TAT picture not included becuase some network issues

ᐅᐅᐅ

Word Association Test (WAT)

How the test is conducted

In this test, the candidates are shown 60 words one after the other and are expected to make a short sentence using the word shown. The usage of the word can be in any form. For example, the word 'agree' can be used as agreeable, agreed, agreement, etc. Each word will appear for 15 seconds in which you have to see the word and write a sentence. There will be a buzzer to indicate that the word has changed. It is important to attempt at least 45 out of 60 words. Do not avoid negative words. Since there is a severe time constraint, you will be unable to mask the responses and your natural self will invariably come out. Hence, it is important to practice. An attempt has been made to provide as many sets as possible for practice.

What Should You Avoid?

- Idioms and phrases that lack the originality of your thoughts and imagination.
- Sentences that tend to preach. For example, 'Don't fight', 'One should not drink.'
- Use of 'I'. I love nature, I am very friendly, I love talking, etc. The frequent use of 'I' reflects selfishness.
- Negative sentences.
- Frequent references to celebrities or known figures.

What is Preferred

- Sentences that reflect your own beliefs and values. For example, helping is a virtue, obeying commands is the duty of soldiers, friends are great company, etc

- Factual sentences based on recent happenings. For example, India is very careful in its dealings with China, or the city of Mumbai faced several bomb blasts in the past. This reflects your awareness
  - Positive sentences.

Two example sets are presented below. Thereafter, five practice sets are given. They include words that are normally given at the SSB. Candidates are advised to time their responses.

Example Sets

1. TRUTH

- Being truthful is the best approch to anything.
  - Truth is always better than lies.

2. FIT

- the street was fitted with CCTV cameras

swimming keeps us fit.

3. BRAVE.

- A brave soldier is also respected.
- Bravery always pays off as god.

4. MOTHER

- Our mother takes care our needs.
- Motherhood is the happiest moment of a parent's life

5. LIGHT

- Future is lighted by hardwork and prepation.
- Light colors soothe the eyes.

6. HOME

- We visit old age home every week to support the old people.
- More than 100 missiles were launched against terrorists, homing in on radar emissions.

7. TEACHER

- Teacher is always second to a parent.
- Ac teacher is like a flame on a non - lit candle.

8. INTREST

- Intrest earned by banks from loans is the source of theiir income.
- Joining the armed forces intrest me.

9. POLICY

- The 52 insurance companies of india have about 29 crore policyholders.
- India accepted the global policies to fight global warming,

10. PAY

- Hard work always pays as success.
- Vijay shekhar Sharma is the founder of Paytm.

11. CAREFUL

- A careful approach gives consistent results.

12. AGREE

- Agreement is essential between the parties.

13. BEAUTIFUL

- Life is beautiful for an optimist.

14. CANNOT

- Humans cannot reach Pluto yet.

15. CONFUSE

- Discussion removes confusion in relationships.

16. BAD

- Bad elements in society require rehabilitation.

17. CROWD

- The crowd rose to their feet to motivate the team.

18. COMPLETE

- A complete man values satisfaction more than material gain.

19. INSTRUCTION

- Clear instruction is the first step to success.

20. CHEAT

- Cheat codes are common in computerm games.

21. SAVE

- Indian soldiers saved people trapped in the recent floods.

22. DOCTOR

- Docter APJ Abdul kalam is regraded as the missile man of India.

23. PREACH

- We should follow people who preach positivity.

24. DUTIES

- It is our duty to uphold india's laws.

25. INDIA

- India is a global face of growing technology and a developing nation.

26. JOY

- I enjoy reading the brave stroies of Param Vir Charkra (PVC) winners.

27. CROOK

- Juvenile crooks should also be tried as adults for heinous crimes.

28. BLUNDER

- We should learn from our blunders and try to correct it.

29. ROUGE

- The army saved the people from the rouge floods of Chennai.

30. HIJACK

- Hijackers are mostly the victims of less self-reliance and poverty.

31. ENCOURAGEMENT

- Encouragement is essential for a child to grow.

32. CRY

- A war cry gives goosebumps to the soldiers.

33. QUALITY

- Quality assurance is secondary in Chinese products.

34. COMPANY

- Good company makes life better.

35. HONOUR

- War heroes were honoured by the world.

36. DEFEAT

- India defeated Pakistan in all the wars they fought.

37. REASON

- Children give innocent reasons for problems.

38. CONVERSATION

- Mature conversation brings effective solutions.

39. OPPOSITION

- Opposition can be handled through logical arguments.

40. DISTURB

- Turbulence disturbs the flight.

41. LAUGHTER

- I always enjoy the laughter of other people.

42. HUMANITY

- We must act against the crimes against humanity as indian citizens.

43. EDUCATION

- Education is the most helpful thing a child can recive.

44. MEDCINE

- Medcine is a rapidly growing field of study.

45. HONEST

- Armed forces is a very adventurous job, honest.

46. CARELESS

- Accidents can be avoided without being careless.

47. ATTACK

- The world is retaliating terror attacks jointly.

48. STAMINA

- My stramina to join armed forces has never weakened.

49. COMPETITION

- Active competition leads to success.

50. PLAN

- We planned a garden in our new house.

51. AWARD

- Awards boost confidence.

52. PUNISHMENT

- Punishment are meant for correction.

53. BEGIN

- A good beigining increases chances of succsess.

54. LEADER

- A good leader cares for his subordinates.

55. WAR

- War causes all round distruction.

56. ANGER

- Anger managements enhances personality.

57. OBEDIENT

- An obedient student is admired by teachers.

58. FILM

- Good films give a massage to the society.

59. ELECTION

- Elections are pillars for democracy.

60. GOVERNMENT

- People's support is needed for good governance.

EXAMPLE SET - 2

1. UNTOUCHABILITY

- Untouchability has been eradicated from most villages.

2. EXPLOITATION

- Poor farmers are exploited by landlords

3. LIMIT

- There is no limit to hard work.

4. ALOOF

- Aloofness can be removed by the company of friends.

5. BLESSING

- Parents' blessings give encouragement for success.

6. HOLIDAY

- Children enjoy the holidays.

7. MOVEMENT

- Rapid movement of forces is important in war.

8. BLUFF

- Bluffmaster is an entertaining movie.

9. EMPLOY

- Women are employed in the defence services.

10. INJURED

- Rush the injured to the hospital.

11. PRECIOUS

- Friends are precious.

12. BRING

- Sportspersons bring glory to our country.

13. INSTRUCTOR

- An instructor leads students to their goal.

14.LIFE

- Life is meant to be enjoyed responsibly.

15. REAL

- Movies and reality are two different things.

16. CLASS

- A class is a group of students with varying traits.

17. RANK

- India lost its Test ranking.

18. LONELY

- With friends around, one never feels lonely.

19. CHOICE

- Choosing the correct profession leads to happiness in life.

20. CO-EDUCATION

- Co-education teaches adaptation with the opposite gender.

21. CHAMPION

- India won the 20-20 World Cup Champions Trophy.

22. DETERIORATE

- Indo-Pak relations are deteriorating with time.

23.CURE

- Ayurveda cures without any side effects.

24. COOPERATE

- Teamwork is all about cooperating with each other.

25. CLEVER

- Being extra clever will annoy friends.

26.DISEASE

- Hygiene prevents the spread of disease.

27. DEMAND

- The people of Telangana were demanding a separate state.

28. FRIEND

- The company of friends gives immense joy.

29.COMPEL

- Indian students are compelled to choose engineering or medical professions.

30.DOCTOR

- A doctor is a god in human form.

31. PUZZLE

- Puzzles are a good brain exercise.

32. FAULT

- It takes courage to admit faults.

33. ENCOURAGE

- Little encouragement boosts confidence.

34. OPPOSITION

- A strong oppositions forms a stable parliament.

35. CONVERSATION

- Conversation improve relations.

36. DREAM

- Dream big to achieve more.

37. METHOD

- Any situtions should be solved in a methodized manner.

38. CHARACTER

- Being consistent and determined helps in developing one's personal character.

39. TIME

- The results have been encouraging enough to trying merit in next time.

40. OVERCOME

- We can overcome our fears by facing it bravely.

41. FREEDOM

- India's owes its independence to its freedom fighters.

42. CONTINUE

- The peace talks between india and with the PMs visit.

43. FIRE

- The policeman fired a shot in the air and controlled the prisoners.

44. CHEERFUL

- My parents always cheered for me during tough times.

45. TESTS

- India has undergone various missile tests to boost country defence.

46.PATRIOTISM

- Soldiers inspire patriotism in every Indian.

47.LIVE

- World Cup Cricket was telecast live on Star Sports.

48. PRIDE

- The Indian cricket team is the pride of our country.

49. FEARFUL

- A brave person is never fearful.

50. PROGRESS

- Hard work leads to progress in life.

51. OPPOSE

- Corruption should be opposed for the progress of the nation.

52. RESPECT

- Indian children respect their elders.

53. BOOK

- A book is one's best friend.

54. SINCERITY

- Sincere work is always appreciated.

55 ALLOW

- Ladies are allowed to join the Indian Navy.

56. GET

- To get success, it is important to work hard.

57.DARJEELING

- The people of Darjeeling are asking for a separate state.

58. TEASE

- Eve-teasing is a punishable offence.

59. CONSOLE

- Friends can console you better than strangers.

60. GRADUATE

- Many graduates are unemployed in our country.

PRACTICE SET - 1

1 BRAVERY
2 COOPERATE
3 ADMIRE
4 ACTIVE
5 CURE
6 FRIENDLY

42 ASSIST
43 ABOVE
44 IMPROVE
45 FILMS
46 BEHAVIOUR
47 EXPLOITATION
48 LATE
49 MOVEMENT
50 CLASS
51 MAJORITY

52 NECESSITY
53 NOVEL
54 EXCEPT
55 CONTRIBUTION
56 NOTHING
57 PURCHASE
58 EXCUSE
59 DISMISS
60 PLEASURE

PRACTICE SET - 2

1 ARMY
2 CHOICE
3 EDUCATED
4 PROBLEM
5 READ
6 REMEMBER
7 RIGHT
8 SCORE
9 TASK
10 UNIVERSITY
11 ENFORCE

45 BATCH
46 ACTION
47 ACTIVE
48 CONFIDENCE
49 DASH
50 DETERIORATE
51 DIE
52 EXPECT
53 HELPLESS
54 LITTLE
55 LOSS
56 MOVE
57 MUST
58 NOISE
59 OPERATION
60 OVERCOME

❧❧❧

Situation Reaction Test (SRT)

Introduction

Situation reaction test in SSB is third test at Service Selection Boards in psychological Testing series, this is the test of candidate's common sense, he/she will be given some situations that occur in daily life and their answers will help the psychologist to judge a candidate's mentality. Situation Recation Test inclines to determine behavioral tendencies, assessing how a candidate will behave in a certain situation, and knowldge instruction, which evaluates the effectiveness of possible responses.

In this test, certain situations are described and the candidate is asked to respond to the same. No special intelligence or knowledge is required to answer these questions. Through the responses, the personality of the person is assessed. This is a test of common sense, reasoning ability and maturity. One learns to act appropriately to situations by virtue of the experience one gains in life.

How the test is conducted

60 situations will be given in a booklet and the candidates are required to respond to these situations in writing. The responses are to be written in a separate answer sheet. A total of 30 minutes is given for this test. Since the time is very short, the candidates write whatever comes to their mind and that is how their true personality emerges. To do well in this test, one has to practice a lot. You may find that one situation is repeated in some other form. Therefore, you have to be cautious not to contradict your earlier response. Don't write merely your reactions; write the full action in short.

Example:

Just before the starting of a doubles match, he found his partner missing.

Reaction:

He took the substitute player.

Complete action:

He took the substitute player, played the match and won it.

EXAMPLE SET

60 situations along with suitable responses are given below as an illustration.

1. He and his friend are standing on a bridge over a river. His friend who does not know swimming, suddenly falls down. He...

jumps into the river, catches his friend's hair, swims back to safety and gives him first aid.

2. He and his brother have gone to a forest; they lose their way and it is becoming dark.

He will identify the cardinal directions with the help of the setting sun, start running in the direction of his village and finally reach home.

3. While going to attend an important meeting, he saw a ghastly accident between an auto rickshaw and a tonga.

He will dial 108 and call for an ambulance, put the injured in that, sendb them to the nearest hospital and reach for the meeting on time.

4. His father has fixed his marriage with a rich girl, but he is in love with his classmate. He has never disobeyed his father. His girlfriend on the other hand, says that if he does not marry her, she will commit suicide.

He will convince his parents about the good nature of his classmate and get married to her with their consent.

5. His exams are starting next week and he is not fully prepared. His father's fast friend suddenly comes to the house and there is no one else to look after him.

He will entertain the guest first and once the guest is comfortable, he will offer him a book/magazine to read till his father arrives and excuse himself stating that he has an exam the next week.

6. His parents have gone to their relatives, leaving him behind with his younger brother. After midnight, his younger brother develops very high fever and there is no medicine in the house. It is raining very heavily.

He will take an umbrella, go to his neighbour's house to get some medicine and the next morning, take his brother to the hospital.

7. He was studying late in the night and at around 2 AM, he sees a man's shadow entering his neighbour's house through the ventilator. His exam is starting the next day.

He will call the neighbour's number, inform him of the thief and also call 100 to get the police. Further, he will call other friends and surround the house to prevent the thief's escape.

8. Two groups are quarrelling over a religious problem. And he belongs to the minority group.

*He will show maturity and convince both not to fight.
Through his mature outlook, he will pacify both the parties.*

9. A fire broke out in the village due to a short circuit at night. He is the
only electrician in the village.

*He will rush to the scene of fire, disconnect the mains and
organise people to get sand and other dry items to
extinguish the fire. Finally, with his direction, the fire is
completely put out.*

10. While studying, he is taking tuitions side by side. But his parents and
friends are advising him to leave the tuitions as he is not getting sufficient
time to study for examinations.

*His financial condition is quite weak. He will continue to
take tuitions, but burn the midnight oil to see to it that he
does well in the exam too. Finally, he achieves both.*

11. While going on a boat in the river Ganga, he falls down in the
fast currents. He does not know how to swim.

*He will start dog paddling and approach the nearest boat,
catch the lifeline of the boat and survive.*

12. He is in the bathroom and has latched the door and is about to
take a bath. Suddenly, a black cobra comes through the drain
and lies in front of him.

He will walk a few steps back slowly, unlatch the door, come out and shut the door. He will call the snake catcher and let the snake be caught and released in the wild.

13. He finds that his girlfriend is moving with his rival.

He will talk it out with her, explain to her the strength of their relationship and win her over.

14. *While going for his exam, he finds a person who has just fallen*
down from a moving bus.

He will stop an auto, put the injured
in it, proceed towards a hospital in the direction of his exam
centre, admit the injured and proceed for the exam.

15. He returns late at night from NCC camp and his stepmother does not open the door of the house.

He will spend the night at his friend's place and return home the next morning.

16. There is a flood in his village and many houses have fallen down. His house is about to collapse and it is late at night.

He will remove all the valuables, take the family members to safety, release the livestock and rush to help others in the village.

17. Some persons are climbing a mountain, but one of them loses his grip on the rope and falls down.

He goes back to searc for his teammate, finds him in difficulty, provides all the support and finally rescues him.

18. He has gone to the coastal area with a group of friends for sightseeing. Suddenly, a storm starts approaching. The tide is rising.

He will alert all on the beach to come back to safety and inform the disaster management group in that city.

19. He is working in an organisation and one of his close friends in the same office is being harassed by his boss.

He will advise his friend to pay more attention to his work, find reasons as to why his boss is harassing him and win him over by sincere efforts.

20. His final degree exams are starting tomorrow and he also has a job call tomorrow. He is in great need of a job.

He will call the company representatives and convince them to change the interview date as he has to appear for his exams. He finally attends the interview on a fresh date and gets the job.

21. He has arranged a party on his lawn and suddenly, it starts raining very heavily. He has a large number of guests, who have already arrived.

He will request all of them to move inside and help him in shifting the items inside and then enjoy the party indoors.

22. He has arranged a party to please his boss on his promotion The party is half way when someone close to him conveys some bad news.

He will maintain his composure, look after the guests and after they all leave, he will rush to attend to the bad news.

23. At a party hosted by him on his promotion, his boss getsannoyed due to the sarcastic remarks of his elder brother andhe leaves the party without having a meal.

He will apologise to his boss next morning in the office and explain to him that his brother did not mean any offence and that it was a misunderstanding. This way, he will resolve the issue.

24. While going to college, he finds that a cyclist has been knocked down by a fast-moving car, but he could not note down the number of the car.

He will pick up the cyclist, take him to the nearest hospital in an auto and come back to the site to see if someone else has noted the number so that an FIR can be lodged.

25. At his friend's marriage, his friend and his father got annoyed due to non-receipt of dowry. They both went away even after a lot of requests were made by all, including the bride and her father. The bride has become unconscious.

He will call his friend and convince him that this is incorrect. He will also talk to his friend's family and make sure that they agree. Finally, he succeeds in his efforts and the marriage happens as planned.

26. He was taking his father for treatment in a wheelchair. While coming out of the house, he slipped on a banana peel and fractured his hip joint. It is raining heavily and no conveyance is available nearby.

He will call his brother using his mobile, who rushes down to help him and finally, both father and son reach the hospital for treatment.

27. In the cinema hall, he is sitting in the last row and watching the movie. Some bad elements are teasing a girl in the front row. He will intervene and stop them from doing so.

He will also make sure that the culprits are sent out of the cinema hall.

28. *He is travelling in a taxi to catch a train. The taxi moving ahead of him throws out a person and drives away.*

He will quickly note down the taxi number, call 108 for an ambulance, dial 100 and inform the police about the vehicle number, put the injured in the ambulance and send him to the hospital and later reach the station to catch his train.

29. He has to go with his friend to play a hockey match in the city. His friend does not turn up and both tyres of his scooter are flat.

He will catch an auto, start moving in the direction of the venue and call his friend to see if he is in any difficulty. On knowing that his friend's vehicle had some problem, he will divert the auto to his friend's home and reach the venue with him to play the match.

30. He finds ten people quarrelling over a purse fallen from a bus. The police have reached the spot. On seeing the police, the others run away and he is found with the purse by the police. They take him to the police station.

He will tell the police the entire episode and convince them that he is not the culprit and that he was only trying to solve the issue. He finally convinces them and comes back home safely.

31. While going to attend the SSB, he loses all his belongings including his ticket and SSB papers in the train, when he went to the toilet. The destination is just 5 km away.

He will search all the surrounding areas in the train, ask for clues from co- passengers and lodge a complaint with the Railway Protection Force. He will go to the SSB, explain the whole thing, appear in the tests and in the meantime, he gets his belongings through the RPF.

32. While returning from a late show, he finds that two boys armed with a knife are molesting a girl and she is crying. The road is quite lonely.

He dials 100 for police help and goes ahead and confronts the culprits. This leads to arguments and before the situation gets out of hand, the police van arrives and thus the girl is rescued.

33. He has to deposit his exam fee after two days, but his friend demanded money today, as he needed it urgently. He is very poor.

He will give him the money and convince his parents that his poor friend needed the money. He will take additional money from his father to pay his exam fees and later, when his friend returns the money, he gives it back to his father.

34. While climbing a mountain, he finds that one of his teammates has sprained his ankle and cannot move.

He will provide first aid to his friend and make arrangements for a short halt till his teammate recovers. After some time, the teammate feels better as the painkiller is very effective and they resume their climb.

35. While going on a picnic on a cycle, his cycle gets punctured in a jungle and no help is readily available. All other cycles are already overloaded.

He will transfer the load from his friend's cycle to his own cycle, sit on his friend's cycle and balance the cycle with one hand till they reach a village where they get the puncture repaired and proceed to enjoy the picnic.

36. His exams are drawing near and he has to cover a large syllabus, but his friend, who is weak in studies, comes to him for help.

He will definitely help him and put in extra hours of studies in the night to cope up. Thus, both of them do well.

37. His parents are not in a position to bear the expenditure, but he still wants to continue studies.

He will take up a part-time job and support his studies on his own. This way, he completes his higher studies and gets a good job too.

38. His mother and his wife are not getting on well and quarrels take place every day; hence, there is tension.

He talks to both his wife and his mother and through this process, brings peace back in the house and a healthy relationship between them.

39. His father wants him to join his profession (property dealing), but he is interested in joining the defence services.

He will pursue his dream and convince his father about his choice. Finally, his father is convinced and he joins the defence services.

40. His parents are quite old and he is their eldest son. The economic condition of his parents is quite weak. They want him to continue his studies.

He will take up a part-time job, support his parents and also continue his studies. This way, after finishing his higher studies, he gets a good job and looks after his parents.

41. His friend is extremely poor, but good in studies. He can't pay his fees. His own financial condition is also not very sound, but he wants to help his friend.

He will help his friend to the extent possible and seek his help in studies. Thus, both benefit and do well together.

42. His marriage has been fixed, but just a week prior to the marriage, the girl meets with an accident and loses one eye.

He will honour the commitment and marry the girl. Later, he gets the treatment done and by eye transplantation, she recovers her vision and they go on to lead a happy life.

43. He is to catch a train, but the coolie has disappeared with the baggage. The train is about to leave.

He will frantically look for the coolie and in the process, he will find him standing with the luggage in front of the wrong compartment. He quickly calls him, pays him the money and boards the train.

44. He lends some money to his friend. Now, he needs this money badly, but the friend is not in a position to pay.

He will ask his father for the money after telling him the facts. His father will understand and help and later, his friend returns the money when he is comfortable.

45. He is the leader of the hiking party, but due to some reasons, two persons of the party want to return halfway through the hike.

He will convince them to stay on and provide all the support needed to resolve the issue that is forcing them to return. This way, they stay on and enjoy the hike.

46. His mother is seriously ill, but his boss has refused to give him leave.

He will persuade his boss to reconsider, and seeing his genuineness, his boss agrees to grant him one day's leave. In return, he promises his boss to complete the work given to him from home and send it to him by email. This way, both are happy. Later, his sister comes to take care ofn his mother.

47. His parents have asked him to return early in the evening, but his friends want to celebrate a late evening party.

*He will return home as there is an important reason why he
has been called back home early. He will convince his friends
as to why he cannot attend the party this time.*

48. His brother is leaving for USA after one week, but he has to report for
duty in an army unit deployed on the border area.

*He will bid farewell to his brother a week earlier and be
back on duty as duty is more important. Later, he maintains
constant communication with his brother.*

49. The river is in spate and the bridge over the river has been washed
away. It is getting dark. He has to reach home with medicine for his aged
mother who has a heart problem.

*He will take the help of the nearby fishermen who drop him
acrosstheir river in the boat. He thanks the fishermen for
helping him.*

50. He is the manager of a factory, facing serious labour problems. His
sister's marriage is after one week and he cannot leave the station.

*He will do everything possible to resolve the labour problem
by convincing the union leaders and proceed for his sister's
marriage. If the problem persists, he will call his sister and
explain the situation.*

51. Two officers, under whom he is working, are not on good terms and
hence, he is getting contradictory instructions.

He will reason with both as to why they should resolve their differences and he succeeds in his attempt.

52. He is returning from a movie. On the way, he is stopped by the police and during the search of his scooter, two packets of charas are found.

He will convince the police that he is innocent and that he has no clue as to how charas was found in his scooter. He will cooperate with the police in cracking the case.

53. At midnight, two young persons enter his house and hold him at gunpoint. They need shelter for the night. Their clothes are blood-stained and they appear to have been involved in a murder.

He will allow them to come in and wait for an opportune moment to call 100 and inform the police. Thepolice arrive and nab the culprits.

54. He went to Shimla on a pleasure trip. There he finds that all his items have been stolen.

He will file an FIR, withdraw some money from the bank, purchase urgently needed items and continue to enjoy his trip. After a couple of days, he gets his items back as the police nab the culprit.

55. The dacoits have sent a warning to the village headman to hand over `2 lakh or face consequences. The villagers cannot arrange even half of it.

He happens to be the village headman's son. He will lay a trap with the help of the police, prepare the villagers to fight the evil and finally get the dacoits caught.

56. While travelling in a bus at night, miscreants stop the bus. They start looting it and two persons start molesting two young girls. The miscreants are fully armed.

He will put up a brave front and pounce on the miscreants. Seeing him, other passengers also join hands and they collectively thrash the miscreants and hand them over to the police.

57. He is contesting the college elections. But all the girls are with his opponent, who is utilising them to snatch his votes.

He would meet the girls discretely and convince them as to why he would be a better candidate. Listening to his convincing arguments, they gradually shift sides and finally he wins the elections.

58. At midnight, he hears a female voice close to his house.Apparently, she is in a terrified state.

He will immediately rushto help her and seeing her struggling with a thief, he willrescue her, take control of the thief and later hand him overto the police.

59. The college students are about to call a strike and they want him to join them.

He will reason with them as to how the strike can hamper their studies and convince them to initiate a dialogue with the college management. He finally succeeds and the issue gets resolved amicably.

60. His best friend confronts him in front of everyone and accuses him of instigating his girlfriend against him.

He will call his girlfriend and clarify the whole issue in a mature manner. Finding that he had not done anything wrong, his friendapologises and their friendship becomes stronger.

PRACTICE SET 1

1.The student of his collage are about to a call strike.He

2. Two of his best friends had quarreled with each other.He will

3. He has had a quarrel with his uncle and he (uncle) decided to leave the house.He

4. His father wants to marry him with a rich and educated girl, but he is in love with a poor uneducated girl.He

5. He has been selected for a good job, but his father wants him to run the family business,He

6. He with six person had gone a cycle expedition and one cycle got punctured on desert stretch of road. He

7. He has quarreled with one of his friends.He.

8. A cobra enters the room at night and start going near his brother who is sleeping. He.

9. While going to the office he find an accident between a cycle and bullock cart, he is already getting late. He

10. He is caught by dacoits and taken to a jungle where they ask him to sign a note to his father for Rs. 2,00,000. He will.

11. His friend hits him. He.

12. He has two offrs who are giving conflicting orders. He.

13. He and his brothers have gone to a forest. He lost his way and it was becoming dark. He.

14. While comming back from the office he witnesses a ghastly accident between a scooter and motorcar.He.

15. His father has fixed his marriage with a very rich girl. He has never disobeyed his father's orders in his life but another girls says that she is in love with him and he has also attraction towards her. He.

16. His exam starts the nest day and he is not fully prepared. His father's close friend suddenly came to his house, there is no one to entertain him. He.

17. His parents have gone to the other village leaving him and his brother behind. At night his brother gets fever and became unconscious. He.

18. He has gone to a picnic and half of the way he finds that all the food packets have been left behind. He.

19. He has gone to a coastal area with a group of friends for sight seeing. there is a stroms and tide starts rising. He.

20. Some people are climbing on a mountain and one of them loses his grip on the rope and tumbles down. He.

21. A function is required to be organised in his school. On the last day, the organiser has fallen sick. The principal asks him to take charge. He is not aware of anything. He ___________

22. His neighbour's son has fallen into the river flowing nearby. Heis not on talking terms with him. No adults are available to savethe child. He

____

23. There is a fire in a girls' hostel located in a remote corner. His house is also located nearby. The chowkidar may not allow gents to go in. He

____

24. He is returning from college on his scooter. An old man asks for a lift, but his rear wheel has very little air. He ___________

25. His mother has to go to a famous temple located in a lonely area, and he has to go for an exam. There is no one in the house and no other conveyance is available on the lonely road. He ___________

26. He has to go to attend the SSB after two days at Bengaluru from Delhi but there is a railway strike. He ___________

27. He has gone for a picnic with boys and girls in two buses. After the picnic was over at 3 PM, he found that all four tyres of one of the buses were punctured and the other bus driver was missing. He ___________

28. After shikar, he and his friends reached the circuit house to spend the night, but found that the chowkidar was absent. He ___________

29. When his turn came in a debate, all the spectators walked away. He

____

30. In the marriage party of his close friend, he found that the food was delicious but ran short. He ___________

31. In the train, he found that some bad elements had stabbed a lady and she was in a critical condition; at the same time, another lady was about to deliver a child and was crying with pain. He ___________

32. At the railway station, he finds a beggar shivering with cold. He is going to meet his relative and is wearing only pants and a pullover. He

____

33. He has gone to receive his friend, but the train is two hours late. He decides to leave and come back later. He gets caught in a traffic jam and can go neither forward nor back. The traffic is likely to take about 2–3 hours to clear. He ___________

34. He wants to organise a cricket match at his college, but his opponent has approached the authorities for a hockey match. He ___________

35. At the college gate, he finds an unclaimed bag. The bag contains explosives, but before he can take any action, people see him with the bag. They are suspecting him and hence want to take him to the police station. He ___________

36. There is a murder in his village and the opposition party has given his name as a suspect to the police. That day he was in the village. He

____

37. He is driving down with his family members from a hill station and the

brakes of the vehicle fail. He ___________

38. His sister has gone to meet her friend in Nagaland. The friend came to receive her at the bus stop. The friend picked up his sister's suitcase and went ahead. His sister was enjoying the beauty of the place. In the meanwhile, she saw 50 Nagas approach her. They were barely 20 yards away. She ___________

39. While delivering a lecture, he finds the audience is not showing any interest. He ___________

40. His friend informed him in writing about his visit to his place, but he, being away from town, did not know about it. His friend went back without meeting him and is quite upset and annoyed with him. He

____

41. He cannot find any job due to massive unemployment. But he is still keen on finding a job and working. His father asks him to join his business, which he has refused many times earlier. He ___________

42. His peon is in need of money for his daughter's marriage taking place after a week. He has some money to clear his dues within the next 20 days. He ___________

43. He is living a simple life. His classmates laugh at his lifestyle and his old-fashioned clothes. He ___________

44. In a drought-affected area, the relief is coming but not reaching the affected persons. He is a social worker. He ___________

45. His uncle wants him to study science and then do a management

course, but his father wants him to do MA. His uncle is more educated. He
____

46. He is walking on the street and suddenly finds that his sister's chain has been snatched and his purse is stolen. Before he could decide on any course of action, one lady has been stabbed and her car has collided with an auto rickshaw. Two people are injured seriously. He _____________

47. His team is to play a match after five minutes, but the players do not seem to be in good shape. During the interval he comes to know that most of the players were given toxic material in sweets just before the start of the match by his opponent. He _____________

48. The question of his marriage created a struggle between his father and grandfather. He _____________

49. He finds that his hostel roommates are not very friendly with him. He
____

50. He is going in a boat alone. He finds a person struggling and i about to drown. He is not a very good swimmer. He _____________

51. A fire breaks out in the neighbourhood. He sees enough people are already fighting the fire. He _____________

52. If, in a group, his opinion differs from that of other members, he
____

53. His roommate in the hostel does not like him. He _____________

54. The vice chancellor is to visit his college to preside over a function. He was asked to make arrangements for it. But now, the charge is being given to another person. He ____________

55. During an army attachment camp, his batch of volunteers declared a strike because of the rude behaviour of a Junior Commissioned Officer and so he ____________

56. He was travelling in a car which unexpectedly broke down on the way. It was getting dark and no help was in sight. He ____________

57. He was ironing his new pants when suddenly he received an electric shock and noticed the wire burning. He ____________

58. He was a member of the cricket team and once, the captain did not turn up for the match. He ____________

59. He was going for an outing with his friends and on the way, he had an argument with them. He ____________

60. After passing his High School, he was forced to take up a job in the railway, but he was not interested in it. He ____________

PRACTICE SET 2

1. He has done something that he should not have done. He is being confronted by his friends. He ____________
2. He is present where an accident has taken place and the mob has started thrashing the driver. He ____________
3. In a play, he was offered a subordinate role whereas he deserved a better role as he was a better performer. He

____

4. He was called upon to organise a variety show in his college. He
____

5. Being in a tight corner when he is called to take a new step, he
____

6. He is tackling a problem which he was unable to solve. He
____

7. He finds it rather difficult to get admission for a study course of
his choice. He ______________

8. He feels strongly that a person can achieve a lot if he
____

9. He finds a person lying flat on the ground and many people
have surrounded him. He ______________

10. He is getting late in reaching a meeting. He ______________

11. His leader has lost his way while taking his group for trekking.
He ______________

12. While sharing a room with another boy, he did not find him
friendly. He ______________

13. He prefers to select Army as a career, but his father is against it.
He ______________

14. While travelling in the train, he finds that he has lost his ticket
and money. He ______________

15. He is contesting an election. To win it, he ______________

16. He is the secretary of the college union, while the president is a
girl from the opposite group. He ______________

17. Finding that the group leader is not working well, he
____

18. He finds that some members of his group differ with him on the
line of action to be followed. He ______________

19. Monday is his lucky day. He has been called for an interview for
a job on Saturday. He ______________

20. Since he has not done well in his studies, he is being scolded by
his father. He ______________

21. A number of college representatives are to be selected, some
by election, others by nomination. He feels that his chances are

not so bright for election. He ___________

22. He has been asked to organise a charity show. He

____

23. He feels that workers in his organisation are not paying sufficient attention to their work. He ___________

24. The group happened to be present when a car struck a cycle. The group ___________

25. He had gone to the station to see off his friend. He heard a woman crying "Thief, thief!" He ___________

26. Two of his classmates seek his assistance while he is preparing for the exams. He ___________

27. While going on a picnic, his friends refused to take part in the music competition. He ___________

28. His best friend joined the company of his opponents and they are making his friend contest the elections against him. He

____

29. His friend is sitting on a hunger strike, but his father warns him not to join him. He ___________

30. He has collected the contribution from his friends for a picnic. The picnic is to be organised tomorrow in a big way. He has gone to make purchases, but realises that the entire collection has been lost. He ___________

31. His favourite game is basketball, but there is no basketball court in his school. The other school is utilising their court for their

own students' practice. He ___________

32. His mathematics teacher is retiring next month, but he was not his favourite teacher. His classmates decide to collect money for his tea party. He ___________

33. He was asked to organise a debate competition, but the students are not in favour of any programme at this stage as the exams are starting after two weeks. He ___________

34. He is the cricket team captain. His college has organised the match, but his mother is seriously ill and his father is not at home. He ___________

35. In his office, his superior gives him a task about which he was

not briefed at all earlier. There is no time to find out the details. He ___________

36. His boss had asked him to do something in a particular way, but in his opinion, that way is inappropriate. He ___________

37. In the examination hall, just five minutes before the commencement of the exam, he finds that he has forgotten his admit card. He ___________

38. While enjoying the picnic (seven boys and five girls), all the boys, except him and five girls, went for a swim. Suddenly, he and the girls saw a wild animal approaching the site. The girls were in a state of shock. He ___________

39. His friend's family members were fast asleep when their house caught fire. He was informed of the situation by a neighbour. He ___________

40. He was returning from work when a truck knocked down a cyclist in front of him. He ___________

41. His parents are out for a week. All of a sudden his brother decides to have a court marriage against the wish of his parents. He ___________

42. He was to carry some money from one place to another and there was the danger of robbery on the way. He ___________

43. While going to the office, he saw some policemen enquiring into the accident between a motorcyclist and a scooter rider. They wanted him to give his statement as a witness. He ___________

44. He was hardly 18 years old when his father had a severe heart attack. Being the eldest member of the family, he ___________

45. His father is a famous doctor and runs a nursing home. He is not interested in becoming a doctor and has failed in the entrance examination for the third time. His father is still not permitting him to change his subjects. He ___________

46. He was out on a picnic with his friends when one of the boys stole some mangoes from a garden and the gardener came out with his stick. He ___________

47. For an examination, he reached half an hour late due to some

unavoidable circumstances. The invigilator refused him permission to appear in the examination. He ___________

48. While his classmates wanted to lodge a complaint against one of their teachers, he did not agree with them. They refused to speak with him. He ___________

49. While on annual leave, he finds that his agricultural land has been occupied by the neighbour. When negotiating, they threaten to kill him. They are notorious people of the village. He ___________

50. He was called for an interview for a job. He badly needed it and it was on the very day his examination was to start. He ___________

51. He is a notorious student in the college. Due to some misunderstanding, the principal decides to rusticate him for three years. He ___________

52. When all the boys of his class wanted to play a tournament, he refused to cooperate with them and they started abusing him. He ___________

53. He has a quarrel with his uncle. When his father was not at home, his uncle decided to leave the house. He ___________

54. He was made the section commander during the NCC camp. There was to be a drill competition amongst the sections. He ___________

55. When the bus overturned during his journey, many people got injured seriously while he escaped with minor scratches. He ___________

56. He was passing through a jungle along with his five friends. All of a sudden, he saw that a tiger was standing at a distance of 10 metres from them. He ___________

57. His fellow-passenger shook him out of his sleep and asked him for some money because his pocket had been picked and his ticket also was gone. The ticket collector had come into their compartment. He ___________

58. While on their way back from the picnic party in the evening, hardly half of them had crossed the river, when the rope bridge

broke. He ____________

59. His father, an army officer, was returning victorious from the war and he had gone to receive him at the railway station. As he was waiting for the train to arrive, he heard a loud explosion. It was the ammunition wagon behind him that had caught fire. He

____

60. They were climbing a small rock and were about to reach the top when they saw the sand beneath their feet sliding. There was nothing around them to hold on to and he ____________

Self-Description Test (SDT)

Introduction

In this section, candidates are given 15 minutes and asked to write five different paragraphs describing (1) what his/her parents think of him/her, (2) what does his/her teacher/ employer think, (3) what do friends and colleagues think, and (4) what does he/she think of himself/herself and (5) what kind of person he/she would like to become or what improvements he/she wants to bring in himself/herself. Most often, candidates write this section without any application of mind. Remember, at every given opportunity, you have to project your qualities. However, projecting your qualities without a basis has no meaning. For example, a candidate writing that his teachers think him to be a very good student when he has scored a very low percentage of marks will raise a question mark. Hence, this section must be realistic and yet at the same time, not very explicit about your bad points. A sample self-description of a candidate who is weak in studies but good in outdoor activities is given below as an illustration.

Illustration

Parents

My parents think that I am a bright child with a lot of skills. They believe that I can do as well in academics as I do in outdoor activities and always tell me to balance the two. They know that I am dependable and for any outdoor work, they depend upon me and are sure that the work will be done.

Teachers

My teachers think that I am a sincere boy with more interest in outdoor activities. They also think that I am good at organising events and can work in teams. Hence, they always trust me for conducting any event. They also say that I must find a balance between studies and outdoor activities.

Friends

My friends love me for being helpful and sincere. They think that I have a good sense of humour and share all their problems with me. They also feel that I am very trustworthy and committed and can do anything for them. They prefer to spend time with me because they think I am an uncomplicated and simple person.

Self Image

I think I am a fine person with a lot of good qualities and some weaknesses. I am sincere and responsible. I may not be a good student, but I am a good, dynamic person and can put in hard work in the area of my interest. I am friendly, caring and lovable and respect my elders. I like to live life in a simple way and enjoy every moment.

The Kind of Person You Want to Become

I want to become a successful person through hard work and sustained effort. As I am good at outdoor activities and can lead a team of people, I want to join the armed forces and become a good officer. I would like to become a person whom everyone respects for professionalism, sincerity and commitment.